All About MY INVENTION

An Inventor's Planner & Journal

October - December

Andrea Hence Evans, Esq.

All About My Invention

Published by
The Law Firm of Andrea Hence Evans, LLC
Copyright© 2020
Andrea Hence Evans Esq.

All Rights Reserved.

No part of this book may be reproduced, distributed or transmitted in any form without a license or permission from the author.

ISBN: 978-1-7343298-3-4

Contact the Law Firm of Andrea Hence Evans, LLC for bulk ordering.

info@evansiplaw.com
www.evansiplaw.com
(301)497-9997
@evansiplaw

All About My Invention

An Inventors Planner & Journal

October - December

_____

(Year)

Andrea Hence Evans, Esq
The Law Firm of Andrea Hence Evans, LLC

DEDICATION

This book is dedicated to all inventors, especially my clients that trust their inventions with my Firm, The Law Firm of Andrea Hence Evans, LLC, and allow me to live my dream and be an extension of their team.

This book is dedicated to my Aunt Glorita McAfee Comacho for her continued support and encouragement.

This book is dedicated to my Aunt L. Marilyn Crawford for setting an example of a strong and successful business owner and mentor.

This book is dedicated to my father and mother-in-law, Meredith and Ellen Dean Evans, for always believing in me.

This book is dedicated to my father, Andre Hence, for his support and feedback.

This book is dedicated to my mother, Bernadette Hence, for her wisdom and confidence.

This book is dedicated to my children, Nya and Austin, who can do anything they put their minds to!

This book is dedicated to my husband, Christopher, for his unconditional love and support.

Thank you Elly Virtually, LLC for your creativity.

ALL ABOUT MY INVENTION

October - December

_____
(Year)

THIS JOURNAL BELONGS TO:

_____

Address: _____

_____

_____

Phone Number: _____

Email: _____

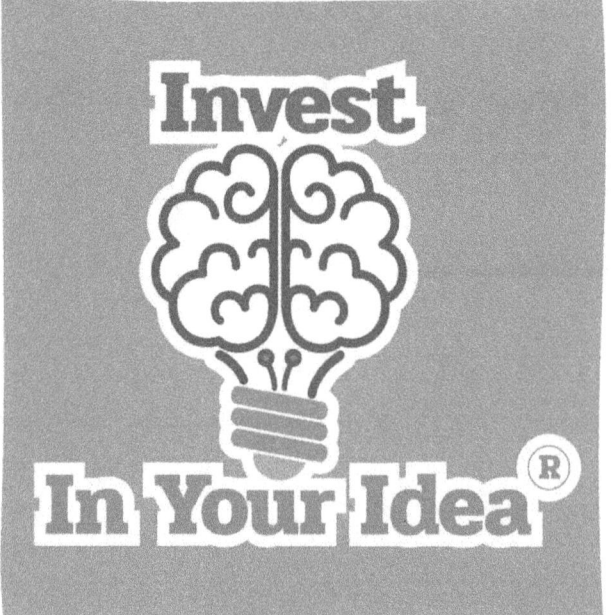

I AM AN INVENTOR!

INTRODUCTION

How exciting!

You are minding your own business and then, it hits you! Your "aha" moment. I am referring to that moment when you realize that you've come up with a better way to do something.

You have figured out a way to make it easier! You have an improvement to an existing problem, now what?

Are you ready to protect your invention?
Is all of your information about the invention in one place?
Did you document important dates?
Who did you talk to?
When did you research the invention?
What is the invention?
Why did you invent the invention?

I'm sure you have these questions and many more!

All About MY Invention: An Inventor's Planner & Journal will assist you in collecting all of your important information about your invention and help you to document it in one place.

This journal combines over a decade of educational experience, work experience, and hands-on patent examination experience to help inventors.

Enjoy

-Andrea

ALL ABOUT MY INVENTION

DESCRIBE YOUR INVENTION:

_____
_____
_____
_____
_____
_____
_____
_____

MY INVENTION SOLVES THESE PROBLEMS:

_____
_____
_____
_____
_____
_____
_____
_____

ALL ABOUT MY INVENTION

MY COMPETITORS ARE:
_____
_____
_____
_____
_____
_____
_____
_____

THINGS TO DO:

- ○ _____
- ○ _____
- ○ _____
- ○ _____
- ○ _____
- ○ _____
- ○ _____
- ○ _____
- ○ _____
- ○ _____
- ○ _____

Is My Invention Patentable?

Here are four questions to ask to determine if your invention is patentable:

- Is it novel?

- Is it obvious?

- Was it made public more than one year prior to filing?

- Does it lack utility or usefulness?

Here's what you need to know about patentable inventions:

1. When you invent something, the invention is required to be useful and solve a problem.

2. The invention is required to be novel or new. If you notice that something already exists that's identical to what you're doing, even if that person has not filed a patent application on that invention, the invention is not patentable because the invention is not new or novel since it already exists.

3. The invention must be non-obvious. That is, would it be obvious to one of ordinary skill in the art, to take what's out there and combine it to make the invention. For example, changing the size, shape, color, material or attaching a button instead of a zipper on something are typically obvious changes such that an invention would not be patentable.

4. If an invention is made public more than one year prior to filing, then the invention is barred from being patented.

MY PRIOR ART

Have you searched high and low for your invention in every store and you can't seem to find it on the shelves?

Don't assume that if you haven't seen your invention in the store, you can patent it.

Prior art is anything that exists prior to you filing a patent application.

Prior art can be a publication, patent application, patent, or even a presentation, just to name a few.

NOTES

_____
_____
_____
_____
_____
_____
_____
_____
_____
_____
_____

MY RESEARCH

PATENTS OF INTEREST:
_____
_____
_____
_____

PUBLICATIONS OF INTEREST:
_____
_____
_____
_____

WEBSITES OF INTEREST:
_____
_____
_____
_____

MISCELLANEOUS INFORMATION OF INTEREST:
_____
_____
_____
_____

MY QUESTIONS

My Patent Application Checklist

Use this section to help you to organize the details of your invention.

The specification should include a clear and concise title of the invention, background of the invention, which can provide a summary of the invention and a brief description of the drawings, a detailed description of the invention, claims, and an abstract that briefly describes the technical nature of the invention.

- [ ] **Title of the Invention**

- [ ] **Field of the Invention** – In 1-2 sentences, describe the invention.

- [ ] **Background of the Invention** – Describe the general background of the subject matter of the invention.

- [ ] **Summary of the Invention** – Provide a summary of the invention in 1-3 paragraphs.

- [ ] **Brief Description of the Drawings** – Describe all figures/drawings.

- [ ] **Detailed Description of the Invention** – Provide a detailed description of all drawings and describe all features of the invention.

- [ ] **Claims** - Draft claim language that identifies the patentable features of the invention. Ensure that these features are described in the detailed description section.

- [ ] **Abstract of the Disclosure** – Describe the patentable features of the invention.

MY PATENT APPLICATION

TITLE OF THE INVENTION:
_____
_____
_____
_____

FIELD OF THE INVENTION:
_____
_____
_____
_____
_____

BACKGROUND OF THE INVENTION:
_____
_____
_____
_____
_____
_____

SUMMARY OF THE INVENTION:
_____
_____
_____
_____
_____
_____
_____

MY DRAWINGS & DESCRIPTION OF THE DRAWINGS

Figure 1

Figure 2

DETAILED DESCRIPTION OF THE INVENTION

CLAIMS

ABSTRACT

OCTOBER

NO FEAR.

OCTOBER:

SUNDAY	MONDAY	TUESDAY	WEDNESDAY
SUNDAY	MONDAY	TUESDAY	WEDNESDAY

THURSDAY	FRIDAY	SATURDAY	IMPORTANT

NOTES

MY INVENTION IS: _____

_____

_____

_____

NOTES

_____

_____

_____

_____

DRAWINGS

I ACCOMPLISHED	DATE	THINGS TO DO
1.		•
2.		•
3.		•
4.		•
5.		•

GOALS	I NEED

MY NOTES

MY INVENTION IS: _____

NOTES

DRAWINGS

I ACCOMPLISHED	DATE	THINGS TO DO
1.		•
2.		•
3.		•
4.		•
5.		•

GOALS

-
-
-
-
-
-

I NEED

- [ ]
- [ ]
- [ ]
- [ ]
- [ ]
- [ ]

MY NOTES

TUESDAY:

MY INVENTION IS: _____

NOTES

DRAWINGS

I ACCOMPLISHED	DATE	THINGS TO DO
1.		•
2.		•
3.		•
4.		•
5.		•

GOALS	I NEED

MY NOTES

WEDNESDAY:

MY INVENTION IS: _____

_____
_____
_____
_____

NOTES

_____
_____
_____
_____

DRAWINGS

I ACCOMPLISHED	DATE	THINGS TO DO
1. _____	_____	• _____
2. _____	_____	• _____
3. _____	_____	• _____
4. _____	_____	• _____
5. _____	_____	• _____

GOALS

-
-
-
-
-
-

I NEED

- [ ]
- [ ]
- [ ]
- [ ]
- [ ]
- [ ]

MY NOTES

THURSDAY:

MY INVENTION IS: _____

_____
_____
_____
_____

NOTES

_____
_____
_____
_____
_____

DRAWINGS

I ACCOMPLISHED	DATE	THINGS TO DO
1. _____		• _____
2. _____		• _____
3. _____		• _____
4. _____		• _____
5. _____		• _____

GOALS

-
-
-
-
-
-

I NEED

- [ ]
- [ ]
- [ ]
- [ ]
- [ ]
- [ ]

MY NOTES

FRIDAY:

MY INVENTION IS: _____

_____
_____
_____
_____

NOTES

_____
_____
_____
_____

DRAWINGS

I ACCOMPLISHED	DATE	THINGS TO DO
1.		•
2.		•
3.		•
4.		•
5.		•

GOALS	I NEED

MY NOTES

SATURDAY:

MY INVENTION IS: _____

NOTES

DRAWINGS

I ACCOMPLISHED	DATE	THINGS TO DO
1.		•
2.		•
3.		•
4.		•
5.		•

GOALS	I NEED

MY NOTES

CIRCLE THE TOPIC YOU WILL JOURNAL ABOUT THIS WEEK:

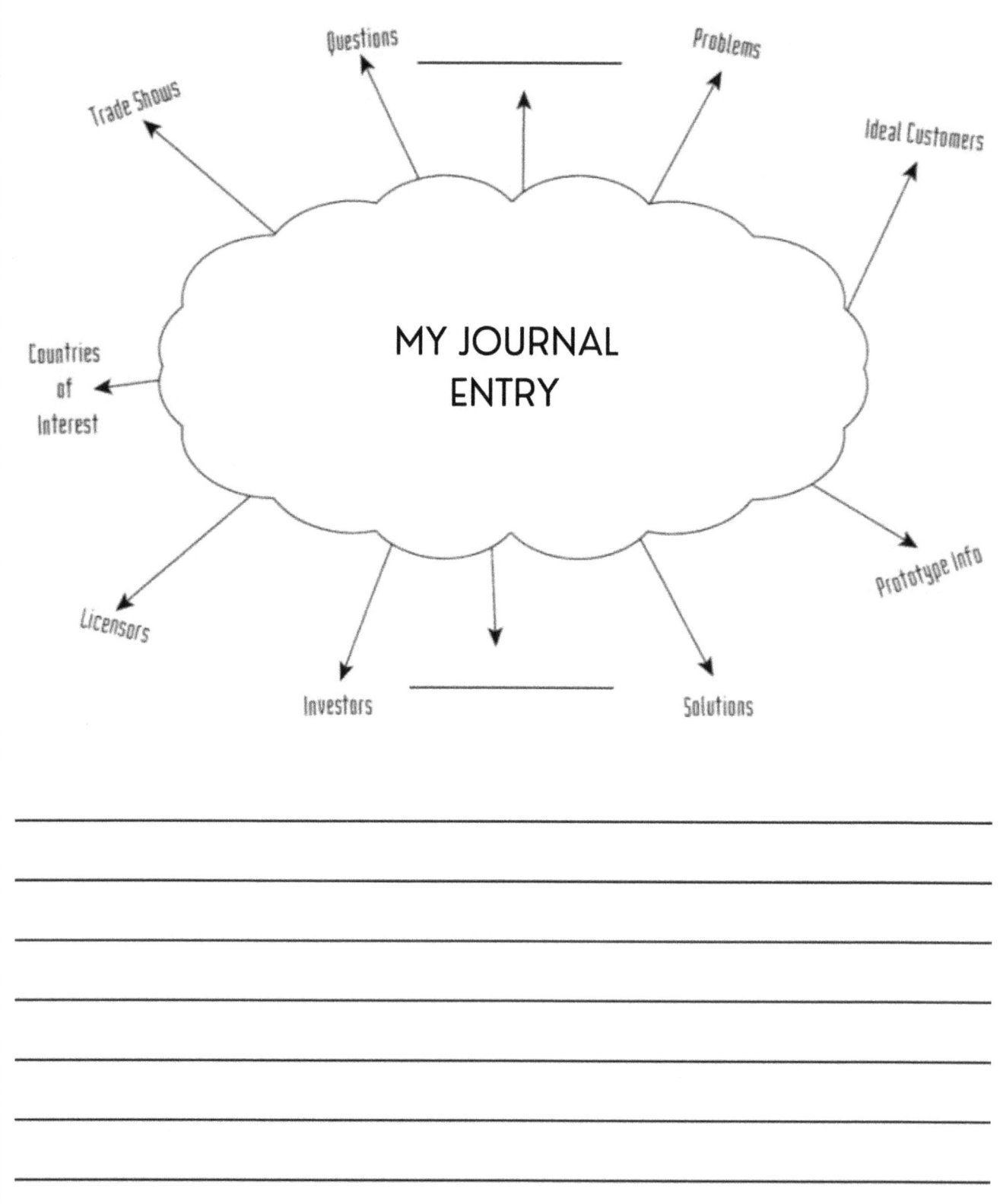

- Questions
- Problems
- Ideal Customers
- Trade Shows
- Countries of Interest
- Licensors
- Investors
- Solutions
- Prototype Info

MY JOURNAL ENTRY

_____
_____
_____
_____
_____
_____
_____

MY JOURNAL ENTRY FOR THE WEEK OF:

MY JOURNAL ENTRY FOR THE WEEK OF:

RESOURCES

REFERENCES

IMPORTANT INFORMATION ABOUT MY INVENTION

IMPORTANT DATES

I SPOKE TO

MISC.

I FEEL

happy sad

worried angry

SUNDAY:

MY INVENTION IS: _____

_____

_____

_____

_____

NOTES

_____

_____

_____

_____

_____

DRAWINGS

I ACCOMPLISHED	DATE	THINGS TO DO
1. _____		• _____
2. _____		• _____
3. _____		• _____
4. _____		• _____
5. _____		• _____

GOALS

I NEED

MY NOTES

MONDAY:

MY INVENTION IS: _____

NOTES

DRAWINGS

I ACCOMPLISHED	DATE	THINGS TO DO
1.		•
2.		•
3.		•
4.		•
5.		•

GOALS	I NEED

MY NOTES

TUESDAY:

MY INVENTION IS:

NOTES

DRAWINGS

I ACCOMPLISHED	DATE	THINGS TO DO
1.		•
2.		•
3.		•
4.		•
5.		•

GOALS

I NEED

MY NOTES

MY INVENTION IS: _____

NOTES

DRAWINGS

I ACCOMPLISHED	DATE	THINGS TO DO
1.		•
2.		•
3.		•
4.		•
5.		•

GOALS

I NEED

MY NOTES

THURSDAY:

MY INVENTION IS: _____

NOTES

DRAWINGS

I ACCOMPLISHED	DATE	THINGS TO DO
1.		•
2.		•
3.		•
4.		•
5.		•

GOALS

I NEED

MY NOTES

FRIDAY:

MY INVENTION IS: _____

NOTES

DRAWINGS

I ACCOMPLISHED	DATE	THINGS TO DO
1.		•
2.		•
3.		•
4.		•
5.		•

GOALS	I NEED

MY NOTES

SATURDAY:

MY INVENTION IS: _____

NOTES

DRAWINGS

I ACCOMPLISHED	DATE	THINGS TO DO
1.		•
2.		•
3.		•
4.		•
5.		•

GOALS

-
-
-
-
-
-

I NEED

- [ ]
- [ ]
- [ ]
- [ ]
- [ ]
- [ ]

MY NOTES

CIRCLE THE TOPIC YOU WILL JOURNAL ABOUT THIS WEEK:

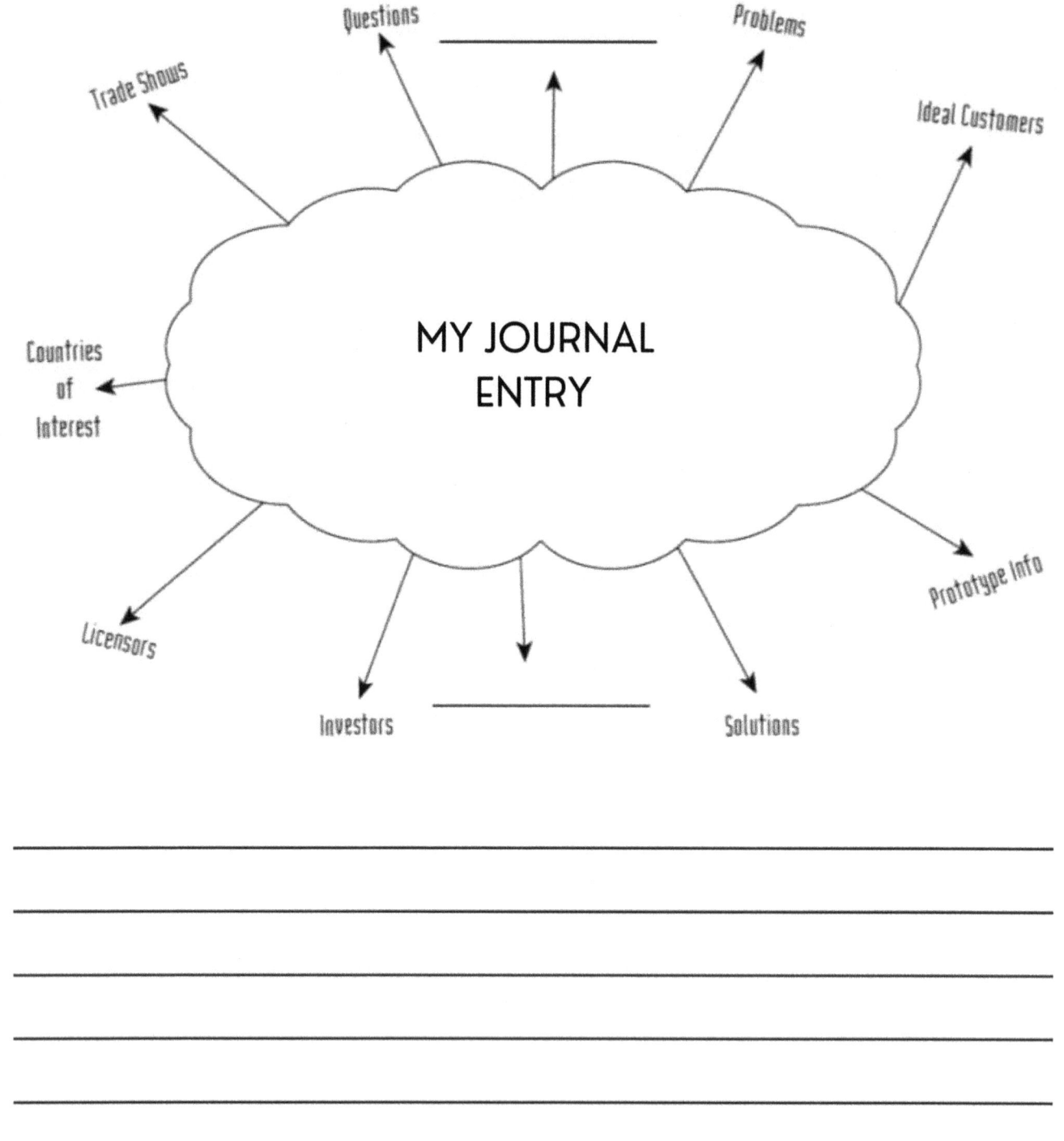

_____
_____
_____
_____
_____
_____
_____

MY JOURNAL ENTRY FOR THE WEEK OF:

MY JOURNAL ENTRY FOR THE WEEK OF:

RESOURCES

REFERENCES

IMPORTANT INFORMATION ABOUT MY INVENTION

IMPORTANT DATES

I SPOKE TO

MISC.

I FEEL

happy   sad

worried   angry

SUNDAY:

MY INVENTION IS: _____

NOTES

DRAWINGS

I ACCOMPLISHED	DATE	THINGS TO DO
1.		•
2.		•
3.		•
4.		•
5.		•

GOALS	I NEED

MY NOTES

MY INVENTION IS: _____

NOTES

DRAWINGS

I ACCOMPLISHED	DATE	THINGS TO DO
1.		•
2.		•
3.		•
4.		•
5.		•

GOALS	I NEED
○	☐
○	☐
○	☐
○	☐
○	☐
○	☐

MY NOTES

TUESDAY:

MY INVENTION IS: _____

_____
_____
_____
_____

NOTES

_____
_____
_____
_____
_____

DRAWINGS

I ACCOMPLISHED	DATE	THINGS TO DO
1. _____		• _____
2. _____		• _____
3. _____		• _____
4. _____		• _____
5. _____		• _____

GOALS

-
-
-
-
-
-

I NEED

- [ ]
- [ ]
- [ ]
- [ ]
- [ ]
- [ ]

MY NOTES

WEDNESDAY:

MY INVENTION IS:

NOTES

DRAWINGS

I ACCOMPLISHED	DATE	THINGS TO DO
1.		•
2.		•
3.		•
4.		•
5.		•

GOALS

-
-
-
-
-
-

I NEED

- [ ]
- [ ]
- [ ]
- [ ]
- [ ]
- [ ]

MY NOTES

THURSDAY:

MY INVENTION IS: _____

_____
_____
_____

NOTES
_____
_____
_____
_____
_____

DRAWINGS

I ACCOMPLISHED	DATE	THINGS TO DO
1.		•
2.		•
3.		•
4.		•
5.		•

GOALS	I NEED

MY NOTES

FRIDAY:

MY INVENTION IS:

NOTES

DRAWINGS

I ACCOMPLISHED	DATE	THINGS TO DO
1.		•
2.		•
3.		•
4.		•
5.		•

GOALS

I NEED

MY NOTES

SATURDAY:

MY INVENTION IS: _____

NOTES

DRAWINGS

I ACCOMPLISHED	DATE	THINGS TO DO
1.		•
2.		•
3.		•
4.		•
5.		•

GOALS

I NEED

MY NOTES

CIRCLE THE TOPIC YOU WILL JOURNAL ABOUT THIS WEEK:

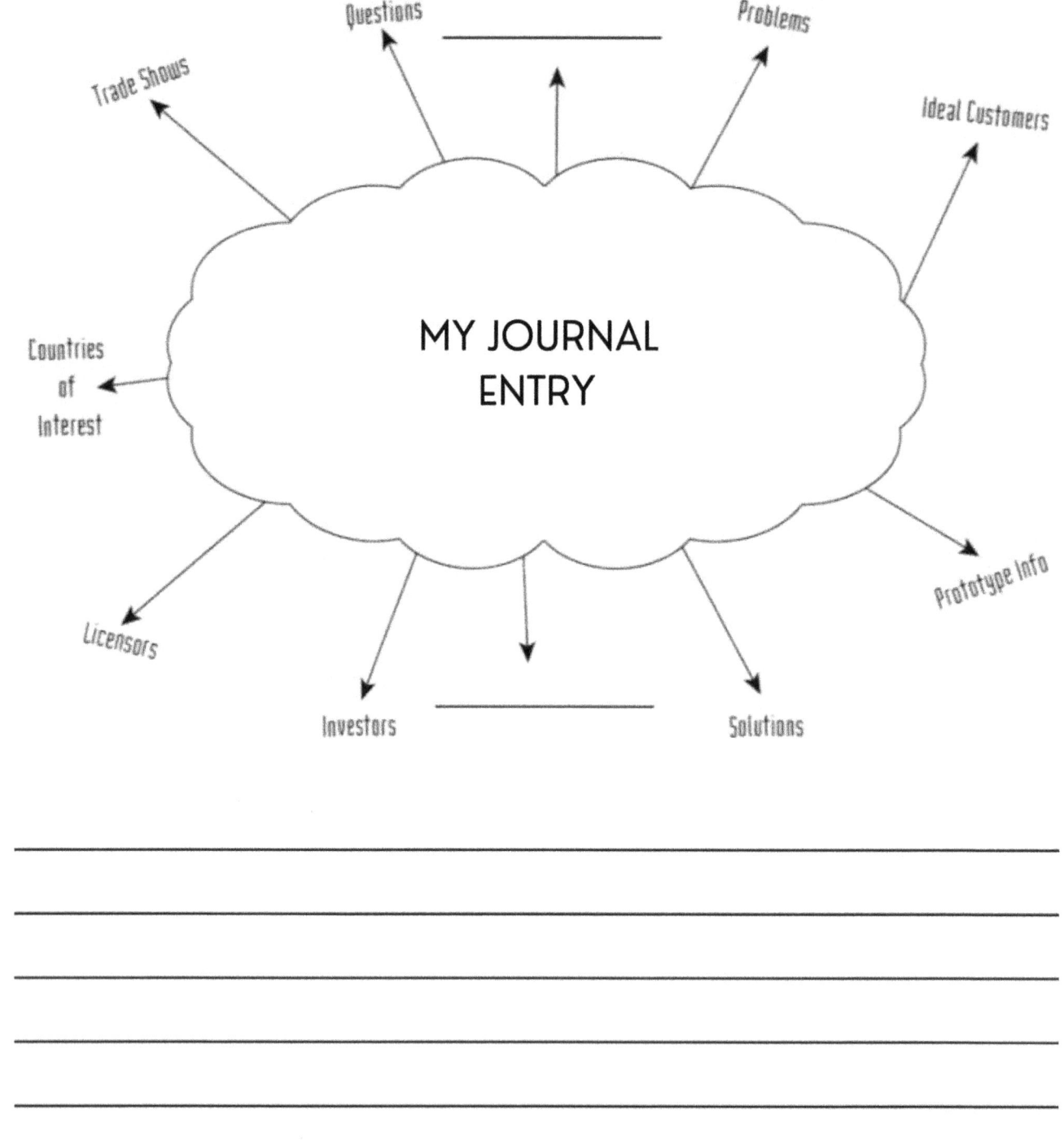

_____
_____
_____
_____
_____
_____
_____

MY JOURNAL ENTRY FOR THE WEEK OF:

MY JOURNAL ENTRY FOR THE WEEK OF:

RESOURCES

REFERENCES

IMPORTANT INFORMATION ABOUT MY INVENTION

IMPORTANT DATES

I SPOKE TO

MISC.

I FEEL

happy sad

worried angry

SUNDAY:

MY INVENTION IS: _____

NOTES

DRAWINGS

I ACCOMPLISHED	DATE	THINGS TO DO
1.		•
2.		•
3.		•
4.		•
5.		•

GOALS	I NEED

MY NOTES

MONDAY:

MY INVENTION IS: _____

_____

_____

_____

NOTES

_____

_____

_____

_____

DRAWINGS

I ACCOMPLISHED	DATE	THINGS TO DO
1. _____		• _____
2. _____		• _____
3. _____		• _____
4. _____		• _____
5. _____		• _____

GOALS

I NEED

MY NOTES

TUESDAY:

MY INVENTION IS: _____

NOTES

DRAWINGS

I ACCOMPLISHED	DATE	THINGS TO DO
1.		•
2.		•
3.		•
4.		•
5.		•

GOALS	I NEED
○	☐
○	☐
○	☐
○	☐
○	☐
○	☐

MY NOTES

WEDNESDAY:

MY INVENTION IS: _____

NOTES

DRAWINGS

I ACCOMPLISHED	DATE	THINGS TO DO
1.		•
2.		•
3.		•
4.		•
5.		•

GOALS

I NEED

MY NOTES

THURSDAY:

MY INVENTION IS: _____

NOTES

DRAWINGS

I ACCOMPLISHED	DATE	THINGS TO DO
1.		•
2.		•
3.		•
4.		•
5.		•

GOALS

I NEED

MY NOTES

FRIDAY:

MY INVENTION IS: _____

NOTES

DRAWINGS

I ACCOMPLISHED	DATE	THINGS TO DO
1.		•
2.		•
3.		•
4.		•
5.		•

GOALS	I NEED

MY NOTES

SATURDAY:

MY INVENTION IS: _____

_____
_____
_____
_____

NOTES

_____
_____
_____
_____
_____

DRAWINGS

I ACCOMPLISHED	DATE	THINGS TO DO
1. _____		• _____
2. _____		• _____
3. _____		• _____
4. _____		• _____
5. _____		• _____

GOALS	I NEED

MY NOTES

CIRCLE THE TOPIC YOU WILL JOURNAL ABOUT THIS WEEK:

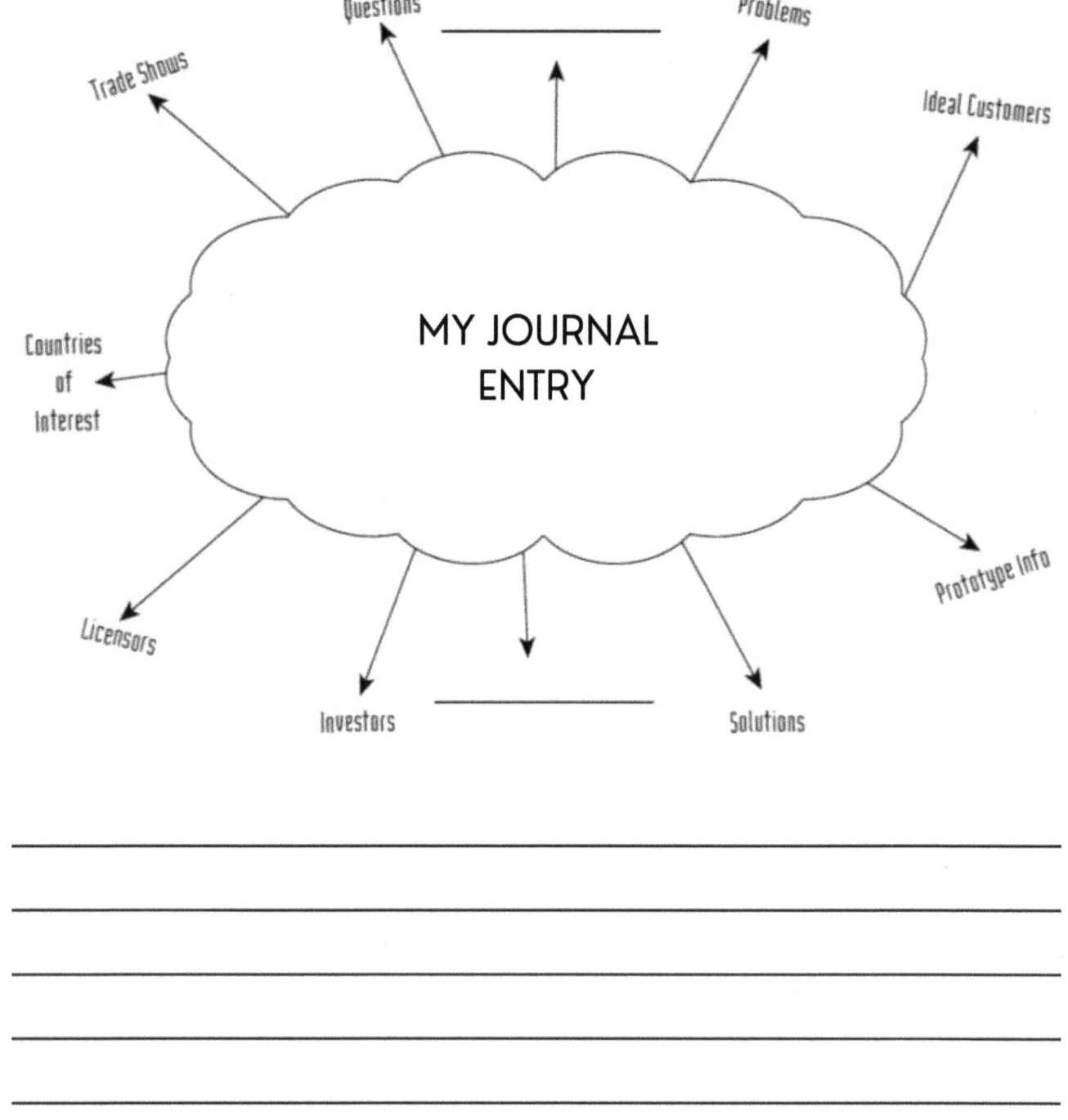

_____
_____
_____
_____
_____
_____
_____

MY JOURNAL ENTRY FOR THE WEEK OF:

MY JOURNAL ENTRY FOR THE WEEK OF:

RESOURCES	REFERENCES

IMPORTANT INFORMATION ABOUT MY INVENTION

IMPORTANT DATES

I SPOKE TO	MISC.	I FEEL
		happy sad
		worried angry

NOVEMBER

THANKFUL.
GRATEFUL.

NOVEMBER:

SUNDAY	MONDAY	TUESDAY	WEDNESDAY
SUNDAY	MONDAY	TUESDAY	WEDNESDAY

THURSDAY	FRIDAY	SATURDAY	IMPORTANT
			NOTES

SUNDAY:

MY INVENTION IS: _____

_____

_____

_____

NOTES

_____

_____

_____

_____

_____

DRAWINGS

I ACCOMPLISHED	DATE	THINGS TO DO
1. _____		• _____
2. _____		• _____
3. _____		• _____
4. _____		• _____
5. _____		• _____

GOALS	I NEED

MY NOTES

MY INVENTION IS: _____

NOTES

DRAWINGS

I ACCOMPLISHED	DATE	THINGS TO DO
1.		•
2.		•
3.		•
4.		•
5.		•

GOALS	I NEED

MY NOTES

TUESDAY:

MY INVENTION IS: _____

NOTES

DRAWINGS

I ACCOMPLISHED	DATE	THINGS TO DO
1.		•
2.		•
3.		•
4.		•
5.		•

GOALS	I NEED

WEDNESDAY:

MY INVENTION IS: _____

NOTES

DRAWINGS

I ACCOMPLISHED	DATE	THINGS TO DO
1.		•
2.		•
3.		•
4.		•
5.		•

GOALS	I NEED

MY NOTES

THURSDAY:

MY INVENTION IS: _____

NOTES

DRAWINGS

I ACCOMPLISHED	DATE	THINGS TO DO
1.		•
2.		•
3.		•
4.		•
5.		•

GOALS

I NEED

MY NOTES

FRIDAY:

MY INVENTION IS:

NOTES

DRAWINGS

I ACCOMPLISHED	DATE	THINGS TO DO
1.		•
2.		•
3.		•
4.		•
5.		•

GOALS	I NEED
○	☐
○	☐
○	☐
○	☐
○	☐
○	☐

MY NOTES

MY INVENTION IS: _____

NOTES

DRAWINGS

I ACCOMPLISHED	DATE	THINGS TO DO
1.		•
2.		•
3.		•
4.		•
5.		•

GOALS	I NEED

MY NOTES

CIRCLE THE TOPIC YOU WILL JOURNAL ABOUT THIS WEEK:

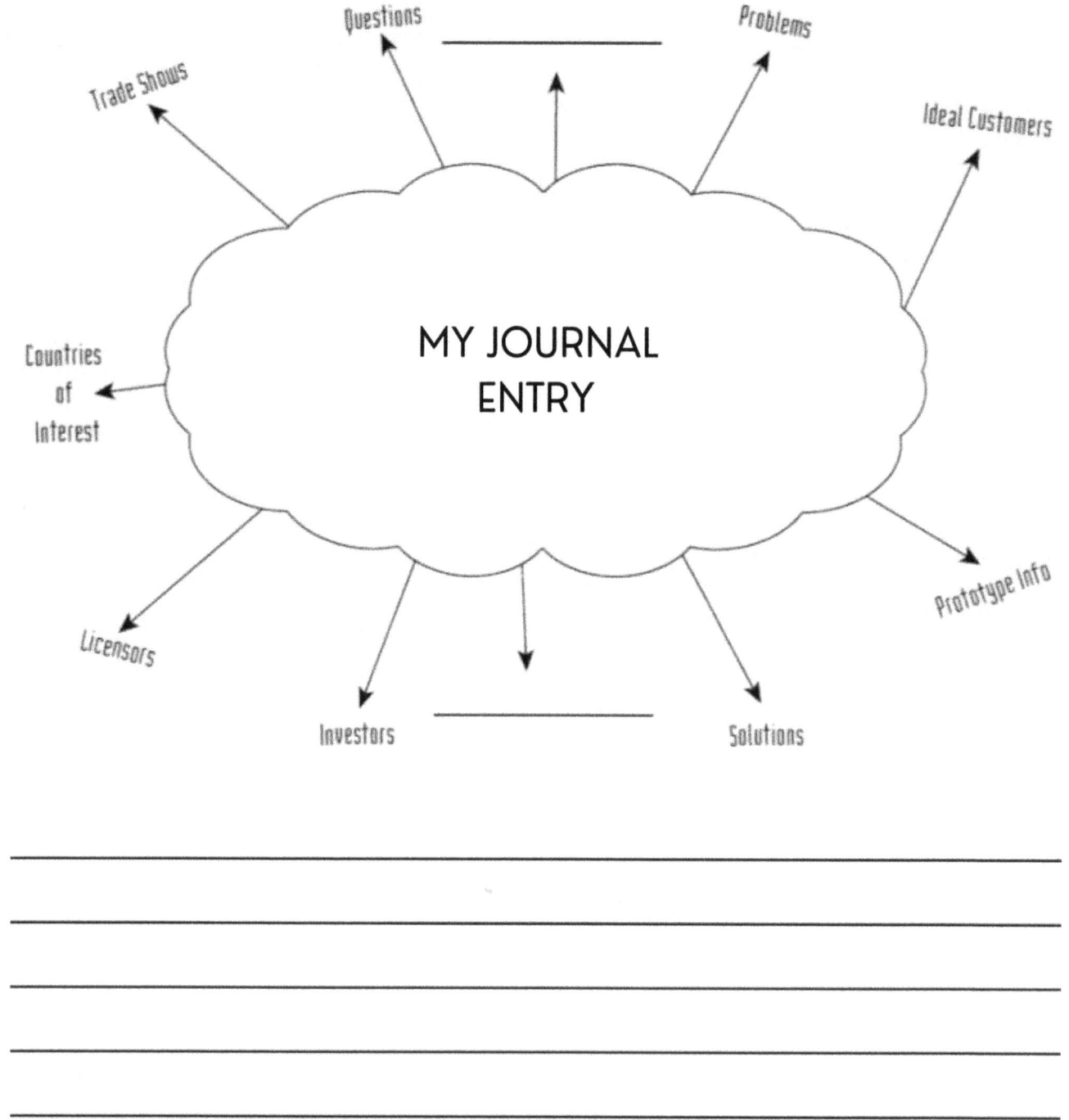

MY JOURNAL ENTRY FOR THE WEEK OF:

MY JOURNAL ENTRY FOR THE WEEK OF:

RESOURCES

REFERENCES

IMPORTANT INFORMATION ABOUT MY INVENTION

IMPORTANT DATES

I SPOKE TO

MISC.

I FEEL

happy sad
worried angry

SUNDAY:

MY INVENTION IS: _____

NOTES

DRAWINGS

I ACCOMPLISHED	DATE	THINGS TO DO
1.		•
2.		•
3.		•
4.		•
5.		•

GOALS	I NEED

MY NOTES

MONDAY:

MY INVENTION IS: _____

_____
_____
_____

NOTES

_____
_____
_____
_____
_____

DRAWINGS

I ACCOMPLISHED	DATE	THINGS TO DO
1. _____	_____	• _____
2. _____	_____	• _____
3. _____	_____	• _____
4. _____	_____	• _____
5. _____	_____	• _____

GOALS

-
-
-
-
-
-

I NEED

- [ ]
- [ ]
- [ ]
- [ ]
- [ ]
- [ ]

MY NOTES

TUESDAY:

MY INVENTION IS: _____

NOTES

DRAWINGS

I ACCOMPLISHED	DATE	THINGS TO DO
1.		•
2.		•
3.		•
4.		•
5.		•

GOALS	I NEED

MY NOTES

WEDNESDAY:

MY INVENTION IS: _____

_____
_____
_____

NOTES

_____
_____
_____
_____
_____

DRAWINGS

I ACCOMPLISHED	DATE	THINGS TO DO
1. _____		• _____
2. _____		• _____
3. _____		• _____
4. _____		• _____
5. _____		• _____

GOALS

I NEED

MY NOTES

THURSDAY:

MY INVENTION IS: _____

NOTES

DRAWINGS

I ACCOMPLISHED	DATE	THINGS TO DO
1.		•
2.		•
3.		•
4.		•
5.		•

GOALS

I NEED

MY NOTES

MY INVENTION IS: _____

NOTES

DRAWINGS

I ACCOMPLISHED	DATE	THINGS TO DO
1.		•
2.		•
3.		•
4.		•
5.		•

GOALS	I NEED

MY NOTES

SATURDAY:

MY INVENTION IS: _____

NOTES

DRAWINGS

I ACCOMPLISHED	DATE	THINGS TO DO
1.		•
2.		•
3.		•
4.		•
5.		•

GOALS	I NEED

MY NOTES

CIRCLE THE TOPIC YOU WILL JOURNAL ABOUT THIS WEEK:

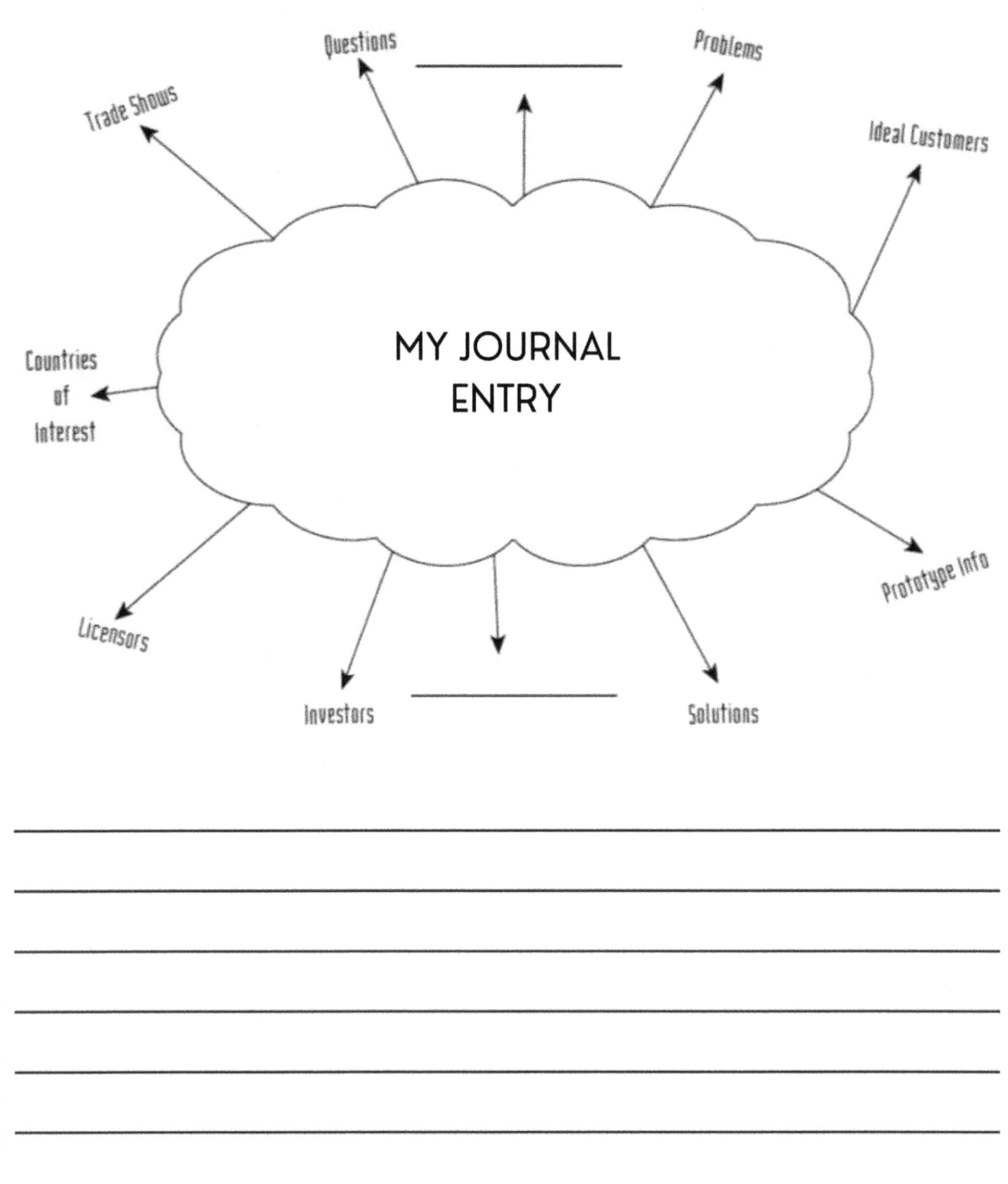

_____
_____
_____
_____
_____
_____
_____
_____

MY JOURNAL ENTRY FOR THE WEEK OF:

MY JOURNAL ENTRY FOR THE WEEK OF:

RESOURCES	REFERENCES

IMPORTANT INFORMATION ABOUT MY INVENTION

IMPORTANT DATES

I SPOKE TO	MISC.	I FEEL
		happy sad worried angry

MY INVENTION IS: _____

NOTES

DRAWINGS

I ACCOMPLISHED	DATE	THINGS TO DO
1.		•
2.		•
3.		•
4.		•
5.		•

GOALS	I NEED

MY NOTES

MONDAY:

MY INVENTION IS: _____

NOTES

DRAWINGS

I ACCOMPLISHED	DATE	THINGS TO DO
1.		•
2.		•
3.		•
4.		•
5.		•

GOALS	I NEED

MY NOTES

TUESDAY:

MY INVENTION IS: _____

NOTES

DRAWINGS

I ACCOMPLISHED	DATE	THINGS TO DO
1.		•
2.		•
3.		•
4.		•
5.		•

GOALS

I NEED

MY NOTES

WEDNESDAY:

MY INVENTION IS:

NOTES

DRAWINGS

I ACCOMPLISHED	DATE	THINGS TO DO
1.		•
2.		•
3.		•
4.		•
5.		•

GOALS

I NEED

MY NOTES

THURSDAY:

MY INVENTION IS:

NOTES

DRAWINGS

I ACCOMPLISHED	DATE	THINGS TO DO
1.		•
2.		•
3.		•
4.		•
5.		•

GOALS	I NEED

MY NOTES

FRIDAY:

MY INVENTION IS: _____

NOTES

DRAWINGS

I ACCOMPLISHED	DATE	THINGS TO DO
1.		•
2.		•
3.		•
4.		•
5.		•

GOALS

I NEED

MY NOTES

SATURDAY:

MY INVENTION IS: _____

NOTES

DRAWINGS

I ACCOMPLISHED	DATE	THINGS TO DO
1.		•
2.		•
3.		•
4.		•
5.		•

GOALS	I NEED

MY NOTES

CIRCLE THE TOPIC YOU WILL JOURNAL ABOUT THIS WEEK:

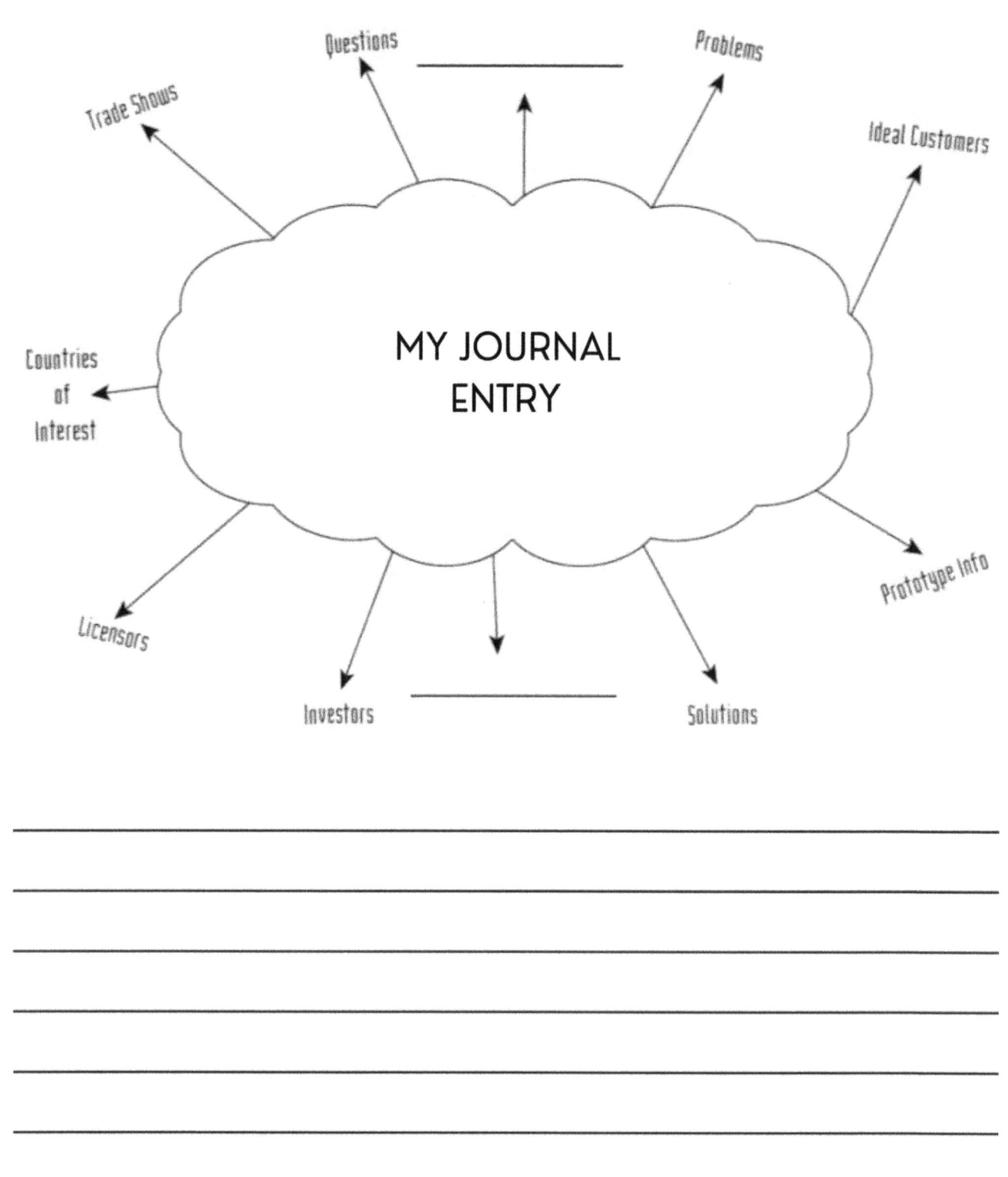

MY JOURNAL ENTRY FOR THE WEEK OF:

MY JOURNAL ENTRY FOR THE WEEK OF:

RESOURCES

REFERENCES

IMPORTANT INFORMATION ABOUT MY INVENTION

IMPORTANT DATES

I SPOKE TO

MISC.

I FEEL

happy sad

worried angry

SUNDAY:

MY INVENTION IS: _____

_____
_____
_____
_____

NOTES

_____
_____
_____
_____
_____

DRAWINGS

I ACCOMPLISHED	DATE	THINGS TO DO
1. _____		• _____
2. _____		• _____
3. _____		• _____
4. _____		• _____
5. _____		• _____

GOALS	I NEED

MY NOTES

MONDAY:

MY INVENTION IS: _____

NOTES

DRAWINGS

I ACCOMPLISHED	DATE	THINGS TO DO
1.		•
2.		•
3.		•
4.		•
5.		•

GOALS

I NEED

MY NOTES

TUESDAY:

MY INVENTION IS: _____

NOTES

DRAWINGS

I ACCOMPLISHED	DATE	THINGS TO DO
1.		•
2.		•
3.		•
4.		•
5.		•

GOALS	I NEED
○	☐
○	☐
○	☐
○	☐
○	☐
○	☐

MY NOTES

MY INVENTION IS: _____

NOTES

DRAWINGS

I ACCOMPLISHED	DATE	THINGS TO DO
1.		•
2.		•
3.		•
4.		•
5.		•

GOALS

I NEED

MY NOTES

MY INVENTION IS: _____

NOTES

DRAWINGS

I ACCOMPLISHED	DATE	THINGS TO DO
1.		•
2.		•
3.		•
4.		•
5.		•

GOALS	I NEED

MY NOTES

FRIDAY:

MY INVENTION IS: _____

_____
_____
_____
_____

NOTES

_____
_____
_____
_____

DRAWINGS

I ACCOMPLISHED	DATE	THINGS TO DO
1. _____	_____	• _____
2. _____	_____	• _____
3. _____	_____	• _____
4. _____	_____	• _____
5. _____	_____	• _____

GOALS	I NEED

MY NOTES

SATURDAY:

MY INVENTION IS: _____

NOTES

DRAWINGS

I ACCOMPLISHED	DATE	THINGS TO DO
1.		•
2.		•
3.		•
4.		•
5.		•

GOALS

I NEED

MY NOTES

CIRCLE THE TOPIC YOU WILL JOURNAL ABOUT THIS WEEK:

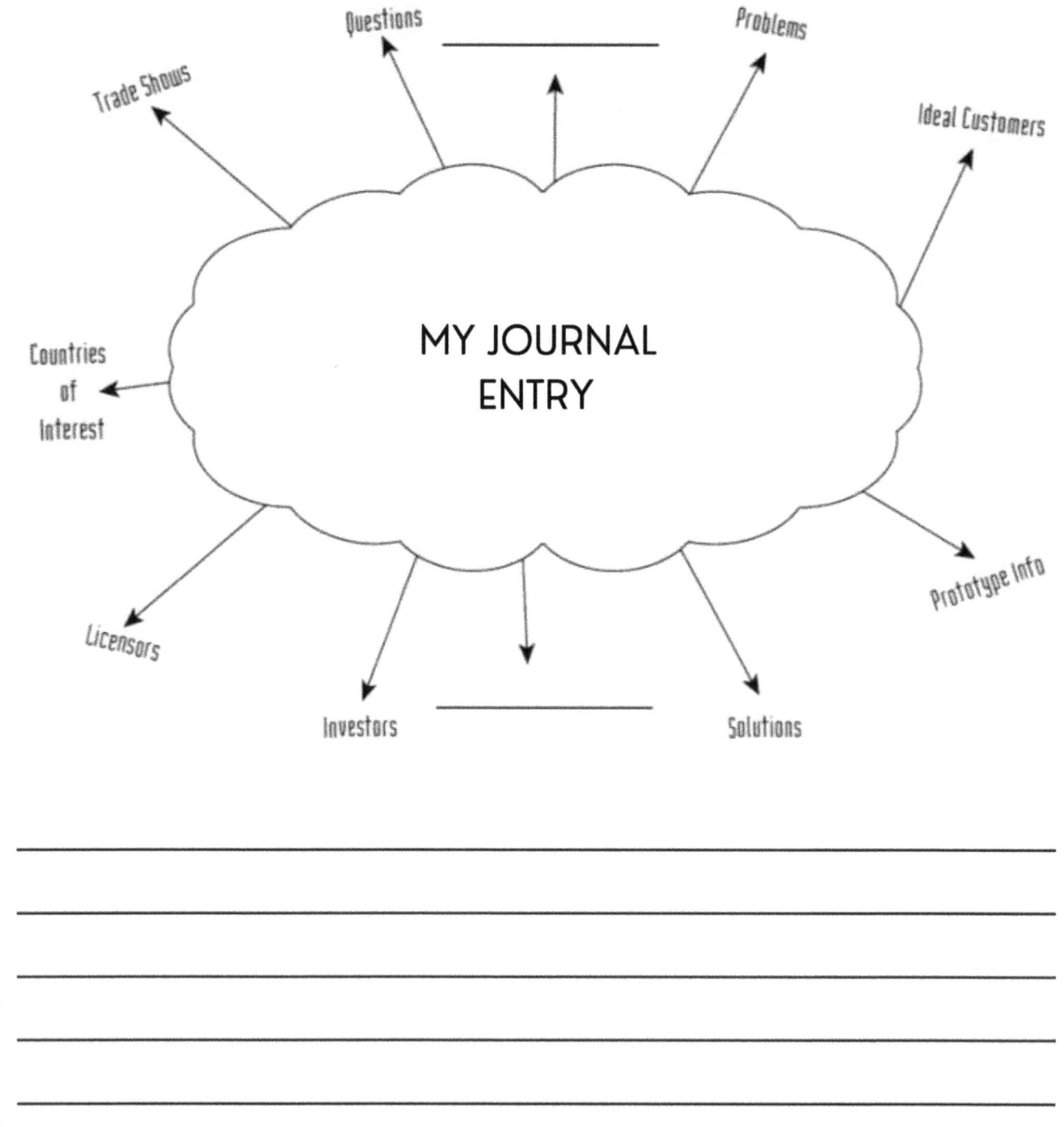

MY JOURNAL ENTRY FOR THE WEEK OF:

MY JOURNAL ENTRY FOR THE WEEK OF:

RESOURCES

REFERENCES

IMPORTANT INFORMATION ABOUT MY INVENTION

IMPORTANT DATES

I SPOKE TO

MISC.

I FEEL

happy
sad
worried
angry

DECEMBER

CREATE. INVENT. GO.

DECEMBER:

SUNDAY	MONDAY	TUESDAY	WEDNESDAY

THURSDAY	FRIDAY	SATURDAY	IMPORTANT

NOTES

SUNDAY:

MY INVENTION IS: _____

NOTES

DRAWINGS

I ACCOMPLISHED	DATE	THINGS TO DO
1.		•
2.		•
3.		•
4.		•
5.		•

GOALS	I NEED

MY NOTES

MY INVENTION IS: _____

NOTES

DRAWINGS

I ACCOMPLISHED	DATE	THINGS TO DO
1.		•
2.		•
3.		•
4.		•
5.		•

GOALS	I NEED

MY NOTES

TUESDAY:

MY INVENTION IS: _____

NOTES

DRAWINGS

I ACCOMPLISHED	DATE	THINGS TO DO
1.		•
2.		•
3.		•
4.		•
5.		•

GOALS

I NEED

MY NOTES

WEDNESDAY:

MY INVENTION IS:

NOTES

DRAWINGS

I ACCOMPLISHED	DATE	THINGS TO DO
1.		•
2.		•
3.		•
4.		•
5.		•

GOALS	I NEED

MY NOTES

MY INVENTION IS: _____
_____
_____
_____
_____

NOTES
_____
_____
_____
_____
_____

DRAWINGS

I ACCOMPLISHED	DATE	THINGS TO DO
1. _____	_____	• _____
2. _____	_____	• _____
3. _____	_____	• _____
4. _____	_____	• _____
5. _____	_____	• _____

GOALS

I NEED

MY NOTES

FRIDAY:

MY INVENTION IS: _____

NOTES

DRAWINGS

I ACCOMPLISHED	DATE	THINGS TO DO
1.		•
2.		•
3.		•
4.		•
5.		•

GOALS

I NEED

MY NOTES

SATURDAY:

MY INVENTION IS: _____
_____
_____
_____
_____

NOTES
_____
_____
_____
_____
_____

DRAWINGS

I ACCOMPLISHED	DATE	THINGS TO DO
1. _____		• _____
2. _____		• _____
3. _____		• _____
4. _____		• _____
5. _____		• _____

GOALS

I NEED

MY NOTES

CIRCLE THE TOPIC YOU WILL JOURNAL ABOUT THIS WEEK:

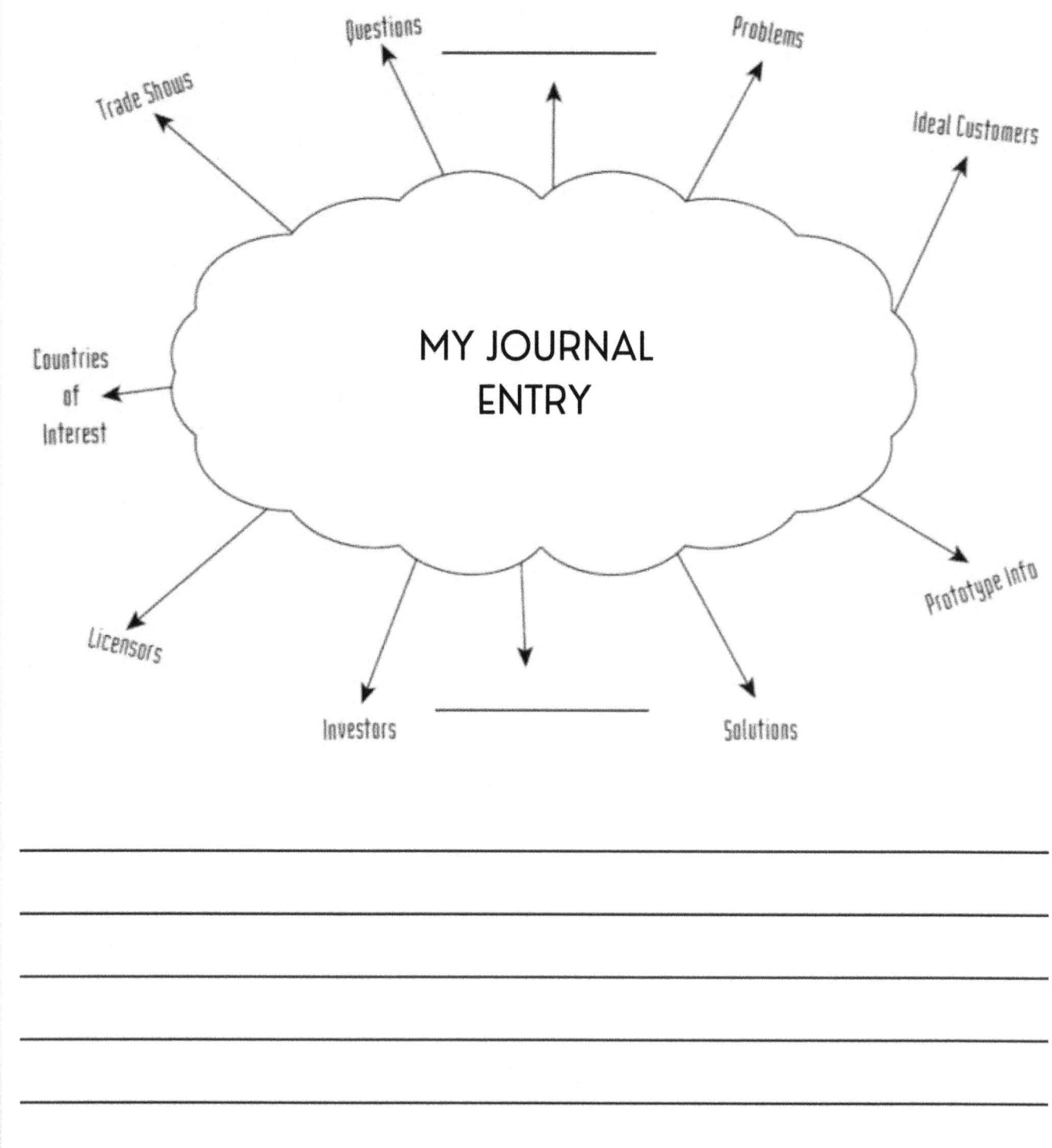

MY JOURNAL ENTRY FOR THE WEEK OF:

MY JOURNAL ENTRY FOR THE WEEK OF:

RESOURCES

REFERENCES

IMPORTANT INFORMATION ABOUT MY INVENTION

IMPORTANT DATES

I SPOKE TO

MISC.

I FEEL

happy sad worried angry

SUNDAY:

MY INVENTION IS: _____

NOTES

DRAWINGS

I ACCOMPLISHED	DATE	THINGS TO DO
1.		•
2.		•
3.		•
4.		•
5.		•

GOALS	I NEED

MY NOTES

MONDAY:

MY INVENTION IS: _____

NOTES

DRAWINGS

I ACCOMPLISHED	DATE	THINGS TO DO
1.		•
2.		•
3.		•
4.		•
5.		•

GOALS

I NEED

MY NOTES

TUESDAY:

MY INVENTION IS: _____

NOTES

DRAWINGS

I ACCOMPLISHED	DATE	THINGS TO DO
1.		•
2.		•
3.		•
4.		•
5.		•

GOALS	I NEED

MY NOTES

MY INVENTION IS: _____

_____

_____

_____

_____

NOTES

_____

_____

_____

_____

_____

DRAWINGS

I ACCOMPLISHED	DATE	THINGS TO DO
1. _____		• _____
2. _____		• _____
3. _____		• _____
4. _____		• _____
5. _____		• _____

GOALS

I NEED

MY NOTES

THURSDAY:

MY INVENTION IS: _____

NOTES

DRAWINGS

I ACCOMPLISHED	DATE	THINGS TO DO
1.		•
2.		•
3.		•
4.		•
5.		•

GOALS

I NEED

MY NOTES

FRIDAY:

MY INVENTION IS: _____

NOTES

DRAWINGS

I ACCOMPLISHED	DATE	THINGS TO DO
1.		•
2.		•
3.		•
4.		•
5.		•

GOALS

I NEED

MY NOTES

SATURDAY:

MY INVENTION IS:

NOTES

DRAWINGS

I ACCOMPLISHED	DATE	THINGS TO DO
1.		•
2.		•
3.		•
4.		•
5.		•

GOALS

I NEED

MY NOTES

CIRCLE THE TOPIC YOU WILL JOURNAL ABOUT THIS WEEK:

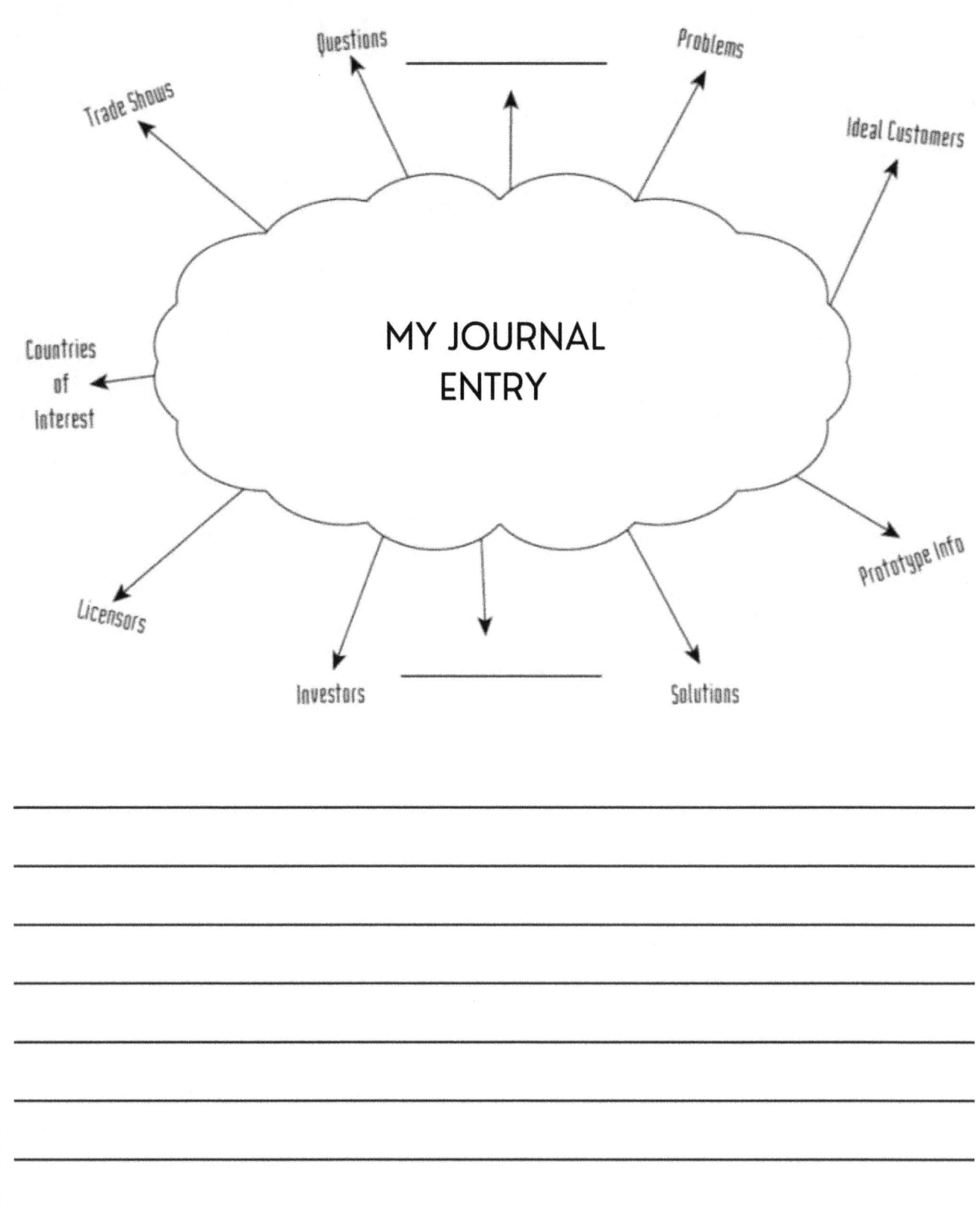

MY JOURNAL ENTRY FOR THE WEEK OF:

MY JOURNAL ENTRY FOR THE WEEK OF:

RESOURCES	REFERENCES

IMPORTANT INFORMATION ABOUT MY INVENTION

IMPORTANT DATES

I SPOKE TO	MISC.	I FEEL
		happy sad
		worried angry

SUNDAY:

MY INVENTION IS: _____

NOTES

DRAWINGS

I ACCOMPLISHED	DATE	THINGS TO DO
1.		•
2.		•
3.		•
4.		•
5.		•

GOALS	I NEED

MY NOTES

MONDAY:

MY INVENTION IS: _____

_____

_____

_____

_____

NOTES

_____

_____

_____

_____

_____

DRAWINGS

I ACCOMPLISHED	DATE	THINGS TO DO
1. _____		• _____
2. _____		• _____
3. _____		• _____
4. _____		• _____
5. _____		• _____

GOALS

I NEED

MY NOTES

TUESDAY:

MY INVENTION IS: _____

NOTES

DRAWINGS

I ACCOMPLISHED	DATE	THINGS TO DO
1.		•
2.		•
3.		•
4.		•
5.		•

GOALS

I NEED

MY NOTES

WEDNESDAY:

MY INVENTION IS:

NOTES

DRAWINGS

I ACCOMPLISHED	DATE	THINGS TO DO
1.		•
2.		•
3.		•
4.		•
5.		•

GOALS

I NEED

MY NOTES

THURSDAY:

MY INVENTION IS: _____

_____
_____
_____
_____

NOTES

_____
_____
_____
_____
_____

DRAWINGS

I ACCOMPLISHED	DATE	THINGS TO DO
1. _____		• _____
2. _____		• _____
3. _____		• _____
4. _____		• _____
5. _____		• _____

GOALS

I NEED

MY NOTES

FRIDAY:

MY INVENTION IS:

NOTES

DRAWINGS

I ACCOMPLISHED	DATE	THINGS TO DO
1.		•
2.		•
3.		•
4.		•
5.		•

GOALS

-
-
-
-
-
-

I NEED

- [ ]
- [ ]
- [ ]
- [ ]
- [ ]
- [ ]

MY NOTES

SATURDAY:

MY INVENTION IS: _____

NOTES

DRAWINGS

I ACCOMPLISHED	DATE	THINGS TO DO
1.		•
2.		•
3.		•
4.		•
5.		•

GOALS

I NEED

MY NOTES

CIRCLE THE TOPIC YOU WILL JOURNAL ABOUT THIS WEEK:

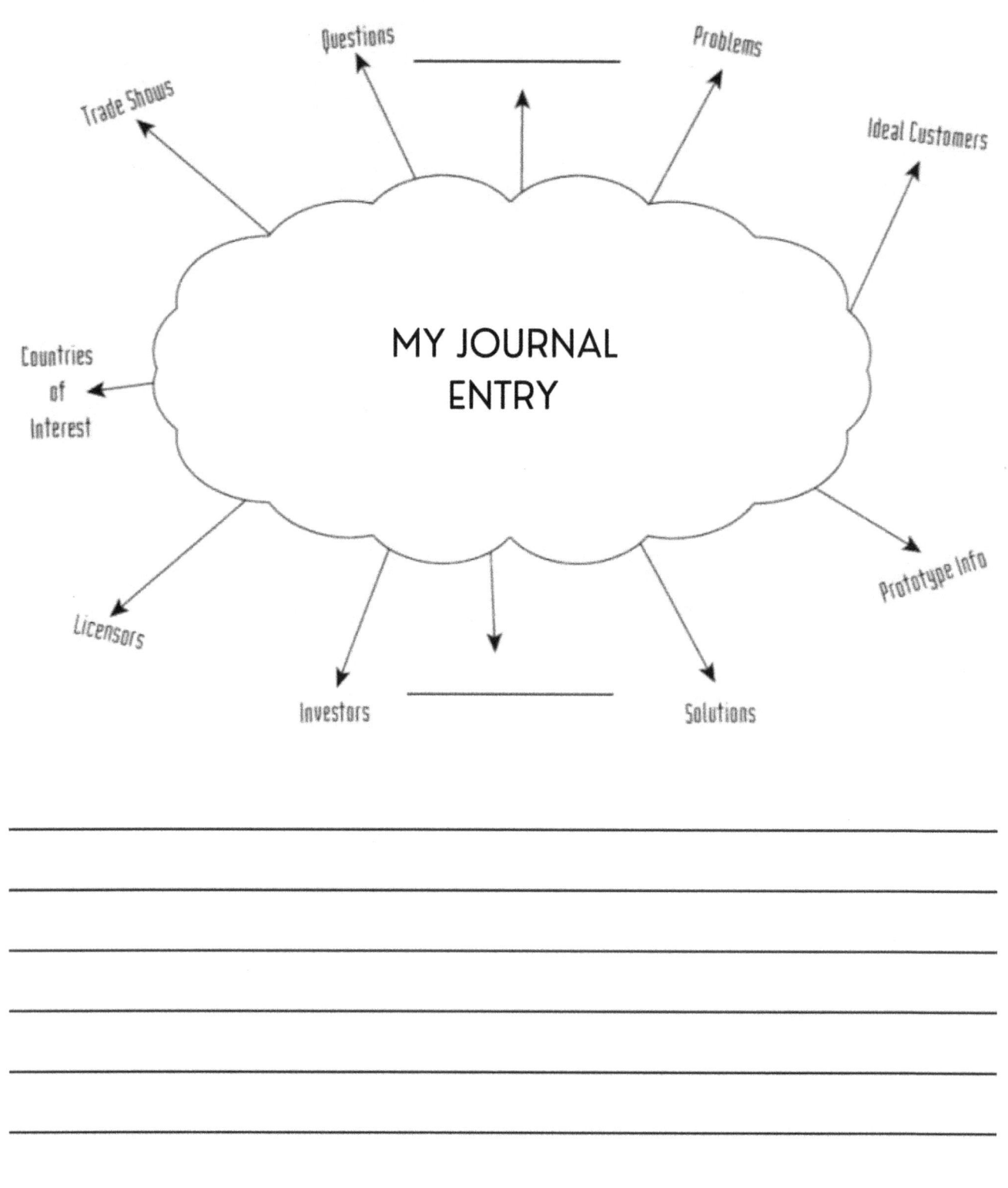

_____
_____
_____
_____
_____
_____
_____

MY JOURNAL ENTRY FOR THE WEEK OF:

MY JOURNAL ENTRY FOR THE WEEK OF:

RESOURCES	REFERENCES

IMPORTANT INFORMATION ABOUT MY INVENTION

IMPORTANT DATES

I SPOKE TO	MISC.	I FEEL
		happy sad worried angry

SUNDAY:

MY INVENTION IS: _____

NOTES

DRAWINGS

I ACCOMPLISHED | **DATE** | **THINGS TO DO**

1.
2.
3.
4.
5.

GOALS	I NEED

MY NOTES

MONDAY:

MY INVENTION IS: _____

_____
_____
_____
_____

NOTES

_____
_____
_____
_____
_____

DRAWINGS

I ACCOMPLISHED	DATE	THINGS TO DO
1. _____		• _____
2. _____		• _____
3. _____		• _____
4. _____		• _____
5. _____		• _____

GOALS

I NEED

MY NOTES

MY INVENTION IS: _____

NOTES

DRAWINGS

I ACCOMPLISHED

1. _____
2. _____
3. _____
4. _____
5. _____

DATE

THINGS TO DO

- _____
- _____
- _____
- _____
- _____

GOALS	I NEED

MY NOTES

WEDNESDAY:

MY INVENTION IS: _____

NOTES

DRAWINGS

I ACCOMPLISHED	DATE	THINGS TO DO
1.		•
2.		•
3.		•
4.		•
5.		•

GOALS	I NEED

MY NOTES

MY INVENTION IS: _____

NOTES

DRAWINGS

I ACCOMPLISHED	DATE	THINGS TO DO
1.		•
2.		•
3.		•
4.		•
5.		•

GOALS	I NEED

MY NOTES

FRIDAY:

MY INVENTION IS: _____

_____
_____
_____
_____

NOTES

_____
_____
_____
_____

DRAWINGS

I ACCOMPLISHED	DATE	THINGS TO DO
1. _____	_____	• _____
2. _____	_____	• _____
3. _____	_____	• _____
4. _____	_____	• _____
5. _____	_____	• _____

GOALS

I NEED

MY NOTES

SATURDAY:

MY INVENTION IS: _____

NOTES

DRAWINGS

I ACCOMPLISHED	DATE	THINGS TO DO
1.		•
2.		•
3.		•
4.		•
5.		•

GOALS

I NEED

MY NOTES

CIRCLE THE TOPIC YOU WILL JOURNAL ABOUT THIS WEEK:

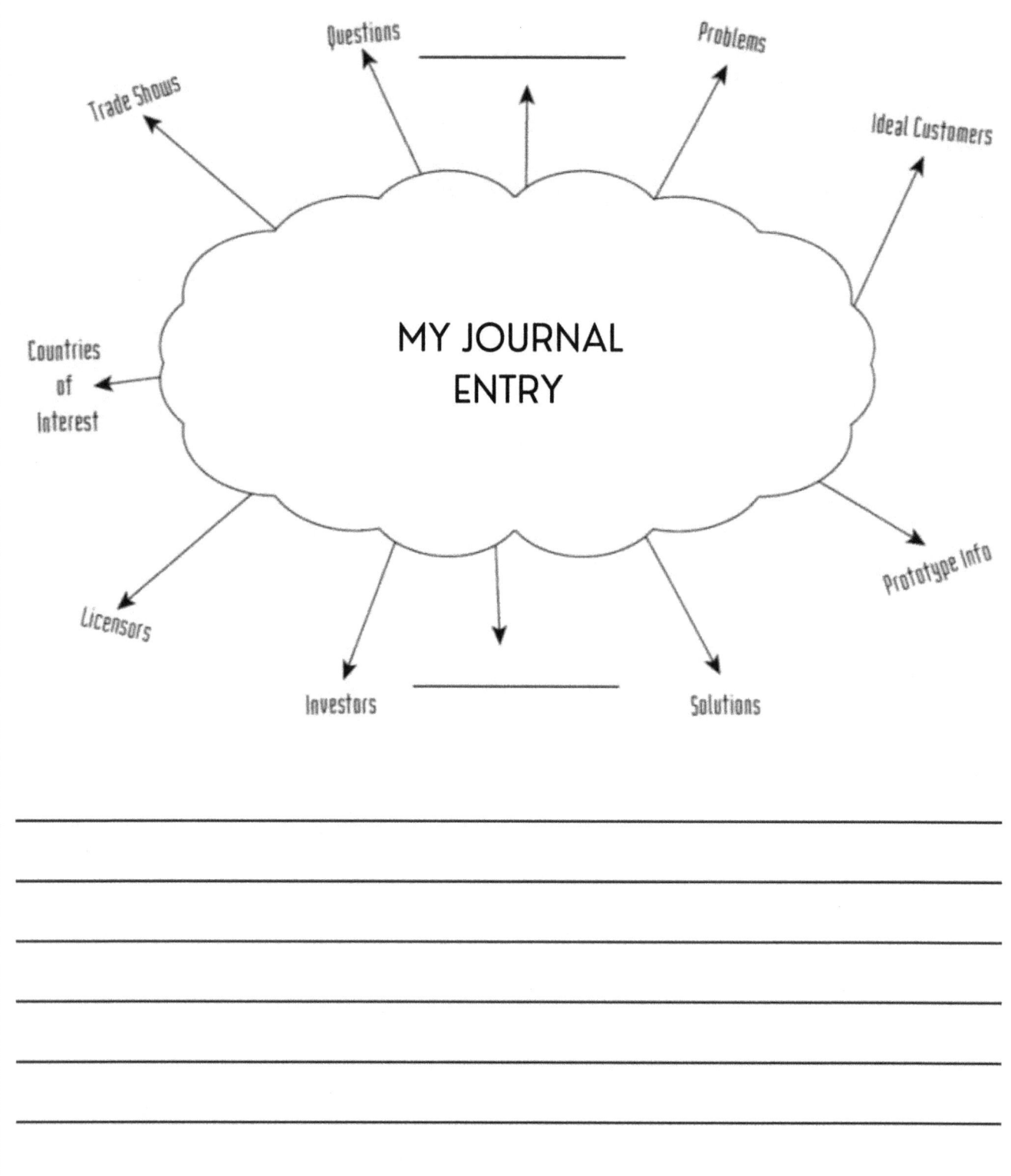

242

MY JOURNAL ENTRY FOR THE WEEK OF:

MY JOURNAL ENTRY FOR THE WEEK OF:

MY JOURNAL ENTRY FOR THE WEEK OF:

RESOURCES	REFERENCES

IMPORTANT INFORMATION ABOUT MY INVENTION

IMPORTANT DATES

I SPOKE TO	MISC.	I FEEL
		happy sad
		worried angry

ABOUT THE AUTHOR

Andrea Hence Evans, Esq. is the owner of The Law Firm of Andrea Hence Evans, LLC. Her career path is unique since she worked at the United States Patent and Trademark Office (USPTO) for approximately 5 years as both a Patent Examiner and a Trademark Examining Attorney after graduating from law school.

Andrea Hence Evans, Esq. is a graduate of The George Washington Law School in Washington, DC. While attending law school, she took advantage of the school's world renowned intellectual property curriculum. She is a graduate of Spelman College and Georgia Institute of Technology (Georgia Tech) in Atlanta, Georgia, where she obtained a Bachelors of Science in Mathematics and a Bachelors of Civil and Environmental Engineering, respectively.

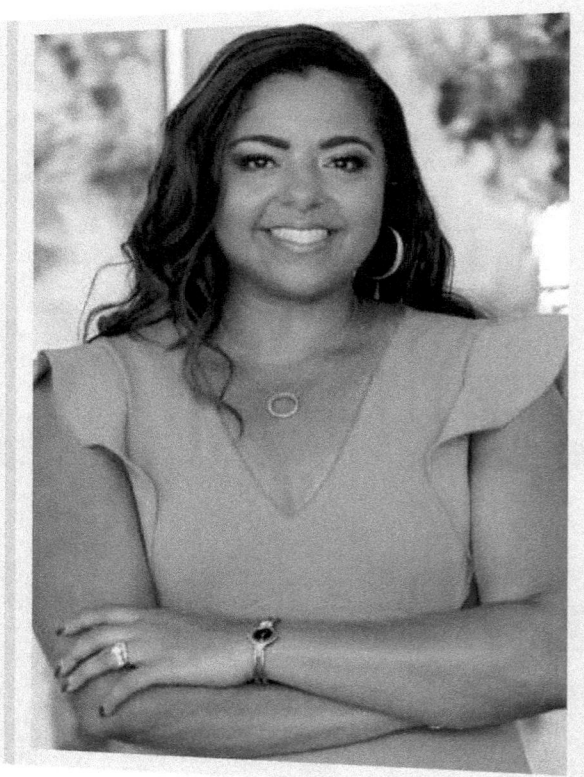

Andrea Hence Evans, Esq. is a member of the Texas bar. She is also a registered Patent Attorney. She is a member of the US Supreme Court Bar. She has won numerous awards and she is a frequent speaker about intellectual property at conferences around the world. She has been featured on NBC, ABC, CBS and PBS, to name a few. The Firm currently represents clients globally with US intellectual property matters.

Andrea is a Patent Attorney on the television show, Make48. She is a wife, mother of two, and owner of KidGINEER, LLC, a hands-on science, technology, engineering and math (STEM) program.

She is an award-winning and best selling author of All About Inventing: Everything You Need to Know About Patents From a Former USPTO Patent Examiner & Patent Attorney and the book, All About Trademarks: Everything You Need to Know About Trademarks From a Former USPTO Trademark Examining Attorney.

Twitter: www.twitter.com/evansiplaw
FB: www.facebook.com/evansiplaw
Instagram: www.instagram.com/evansiplaw
Website: www.evansiplaw.com
Email: info@evansiplaw.com
(301) 497-9997

CPSIA information can be obtained
at www.ICGtesting.com
Printed in the USA
LVHW062041150920
665717LV00004B/14

9 781734 329834